Inside the NFL

Indianapolis Colts

BY
ZACH WYNER

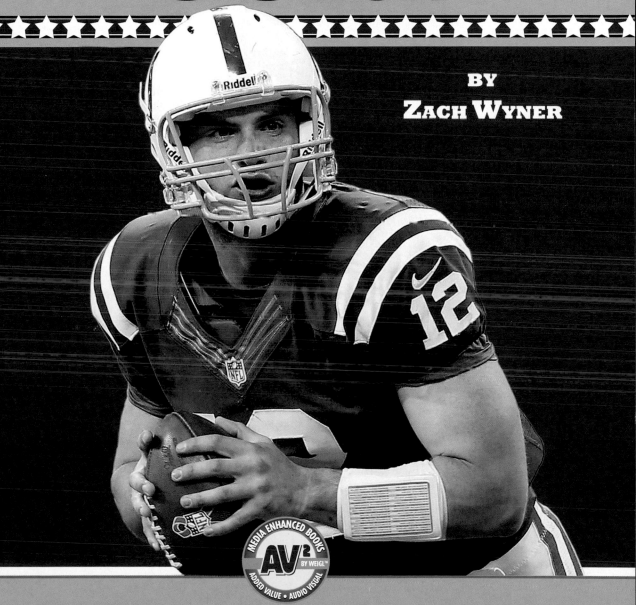

www.av2books.com

AV² provides enriched content that supplements and complements this book. Weigl's AV² books strive to create inspired learning and engage young minds in a total learning experience.

Your AV² Media Enhanced books come alive with...

Audio
Listen to sections of the book read aloud.

Key Words
Study vocabulary, and complete a matching word activity.

Video
Watch informative video clips.

Quizzes
Test your knowledge.

Embedded Weblinks
Gain additional information for research.

Slide Show
View images and captions, and prepare a presentation.

Try This!
Complete activities and hands-on experiments.

... and much, much more!

Go to **www.av2books.com**, and enter this book's unique code.

BOOK CODE

J972050

AV² by Weigl brings you media enhanced books that support active learning.

Published by AV² by Weigl
350 5ᵗʰ Avenue, 59ᵗʰ Floor
New York, NY 10118
Websites: www.av2books.com   www.weigl.com

Library of Congress Control Number: 2014930848

ISBN 978-1-4896-0834-5 (hardcover)
ISBN 978-1-4896-0836-9 (single user ebook)
ISBN 978-1-4896-0837-6 (multi user ebook)

Printed in the United States of America in North Mankato, Minnesota
1 2 3 4 5 6 7 8 9 0   18 17 16 15 14

042014
WEP150314

Project Coordinator Aaron Carr
Art Director Terry Paulhus

Photo Credits
Every reasonable effort has been made to trace ownership and to obtain permission to reprint copyright material. The publishers would be pleased to have any errors or omissions brought to their attention so that they may be corrected in subsequent printings.

Weigl acknowledges Getty Images as its primary image supplier for this title.

Indianapolis Colts

CONTENTS

Introduction

Indianapolis is a hub of sporting activity. From the Indianapolis 500 to college basketball's Final Four, the city's mega-events attract millions of tourists every year. Indiana's love of basketball dates back more than a century. Nonetheless, no current Indiana sports franchise is more loved than the Indianapolis Colts.

Originally from Baltimore, Maryland, the Colts enjoyed incredible success before moving to Indiana. Winners of two National Football League (NFL) Championships in the 1950s and a **Super Bowl** title in 1970, their list of Pro Football **Hall of Fame** players included names like Johnny Unitas, Art Donovan, Gino Marchetti, and Lenny Moore. However, with the Colts making the **playoffs** just once in their first 11 years in Indianapolis, it seemed that their days of dominance were done.

The Colts have had a history of great quarterbacks, including Johnny Unitas and Peyton Manning.

Then, the Colts drafted a young quarterback out of the University of Tennessee and started a run of success the likes of which the NFL has rarely seen.

Andrew Luck is the current starting quarterback of the Colts. He was drafted by Indianapolis in 2012.

COLTS

Stadium Lucas Oil Stadium

Division American Football Conference (AFC) South

Head coach Chuck Pagano

Location Indianapolis, Indiana

NFL championships 1958, 1959, 1968, 1970, 2006

Nicknames The Sack Pack, The Cardiac Colts

26
Playoff Appearances

5
NFL Championships

15
Division Championships

History

2003–2010

The Colts were

DIVISION CHAMPIONS

in every season but one (2008).

Johnny Unitas played for the Colts during three decades, from 1956 to 1972.

n 1953, the Baltimore Colts became the 12th NFL team. Three years later, Johnny Unitas arrived, and the Colts rose to the top of the NFL's Western Conference. In the 1958 NFL Championship Game, they beat the New York Giants, 23–17, in a game remembered as one of the greatest ever played. Unitas and a host of other stars would lead the Colts to four NFL Championships in 13 seasons. However, by the time the Colts arrived in Indianapolis in 1984, those victories were in the past. The Colts had not won a playoff game since 1971.

After a rocky start in Indianapolis, the Colts traded for Eric Dickerson, the future hall of fame running back from the Los Angeles Rams. They made the playoffs in 1987 and hovered around **.500** for the next few years. Then, the wheels came off, as the Colts tumbled to a 1-15 win-loss record in 1991.

In the mid-1990s, Jim Harbaugh and Marshall Faulk spurred a Colts rebirth. By 1997, however, the Colts had again fallen on hard times. They used the first pick in the 1998 **NFL Draft** to select Peyton Manning. In 13 seasons, Manning would lead the Colts to 11 playoff appearances and a Super Bowl title.

└ Peyton Manning was named the best football player of the 2000s by *Sports Illustrated*.

The Stadium

When Lucas Oil Stadium's roof is closed, it amplifies the already loud crowd.

Lucas Oil Stadium features the latest technology. Known as "The House That Manning Built," because of Peyton Manning's importance to Indianapolis football, it was constructed using kinesthetic architecture. This means that it can quickly change form in order to meet the needs of a variety of events such as football, basketball, soccer, and public concerts.

⅃ Many Colts fans wear extreme costumes on game day.

One of Lucas Oil Stadium's many moving parts is the roof. The roof is gabled, meaning that its center is its highest peak. When the weather is nice, the roof's **retractable** panels slide down the slope in order to expose the playing field to the weather. Its unique design enables it to make the largest opening to the sky of any retractable roof in the country. The stadium also features a large, movable window wall at its northern end that allows additional light inside and creates greater airflow when opened.

The Colts have had remarkable success at Lucas Oil Stadium. In fact, since the stadium's opening, division rivals Houston and Tennessee have not won a single game played there.

⅃ While taking in a game at Lucas Oil Stadium, hungry Colts fans feast on home-style pot roast sandwiches.

Where They Play

CANADA

Washington
Oregon
Montana
North Dakota
Minnesota
Lake Superior

Idaho
South Dakota
Wyoming
Wisconsin

Nevada
Utah
Nebraska
Iowa
Illinois

California
Colorado
Kansas
Missouri

UNITED STATES

Arizona
New Mexico
Oklahoma
Arkansas

Pacific Ocean

Texas
Louisiana
Mississip[pi]

Alaska

0 500 Miles
0 500 km

Hawai'i

0 100 Miles
0 100 km

MEXICO

Gulf of Mexico

30 29 15 16 14 23 22 24 13 31 32 17 12 27

AMERICAN FOOTBALL CONFERENCE

EAST		NORTH		SOUTH		WEST	
1	Gillette Stadium	5	FirstEnergy Stadium	9	EverBank Field	13	Arrowhead Stadium
2	MetLife Stadium	6	Heinz Field	10	LP Field	14	Sports Authority Field at Mile High
3	Ralph Wilson Stadium	7	M&T Bank Stadium	★11	Lucas Oil Stadium	15	O.co Coliseum
4	Sun Life Stadium	8	Paul Brown Stadium	12	NRG Stadium	16	Qualcomm Stadium

LUCAS OIL
STADIUM

Location
500 South Capitol Avenue
Indianapolis, Indiana

Broke ground
September 20, 2005

Completed
August 16, 2008

Surface
FieldTurf artificial playing surface

Features
- retractable roof
- 137 luxury suites
- Quarterback Suite, which seats up to 200 people
- two huge 97 by 53 feet (29.6 by 16.2 meters) high-definition scoreboards

LEGEND
American Football Conference
National Football Conference
Lucas Oil Stadium

Lake Michigan
Lake Huron
Lake Ontario
Lake Erie

New Hampshire
Maine
Vermont
New York
Massachusetts
Rhode Island
Connecticut
Michigan
Pennsylvania
New Jersey
Ohio
Delaware
Maryland
West Virginia
Virginia
Kentucky
North Carolina
South Carolina
Georgia
Alabama
Tennessee
Indiana
Florida

Atlantic Ocean

0   250 Miles
0   250 Kilometers

N

NATIONAL FOOTBALL CONFERENCE

EAST	NORTH	SOUTH	WEST
17 AT&T Stadium	21 Ford Field	25 Bank of America Stadium	29 Levi's Stadium
18 FedExField	22 Lambeau Field	26 Georgia Dome	30 CenturyLink Field
19 Lincoln Financial Field	23 Mall of America Field	27 Mercedes-Benz Superdome	31 Edward Jones Dome
20 MetLife Stadium	24 Soldier Field	28 Raymond James Stadium	32 University of Phoenix Stadium

The Uniforms

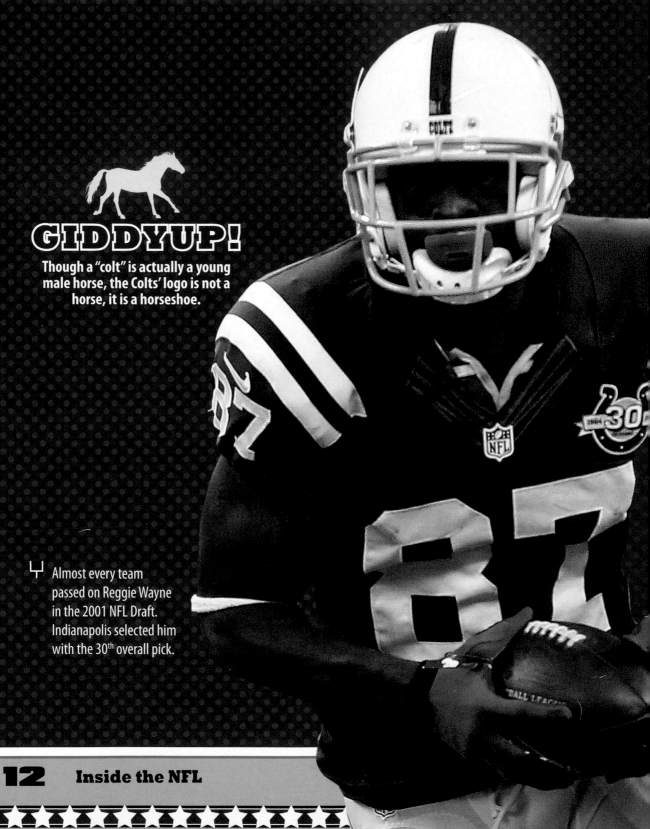

GIDDYUP!

Though a "colt" is actually a young male horse, the Colts' logo is not a horse, it is a horseshoe.

ᒥ Almost every team passed on Reggie Wayne in the 2001 NFL Draft. Indianapolis selected him with the 30th overall pick.

Very little about the Colts' uniforms has changed since the team's debut in 1953. The original uniforms were white with blue stripes and blue numbers on the front and back, or blue with white stripes and white numbers. The one major difference in their **inaugural** season was that at night they wore red jerseys.

HOME

AWAY

In 2002, the Colts changed the striping pattern on their shoulders. The stripe appeared only on the top of the shoulder instead of continuing all the way around. The change was made in an effort to reduce the amount of material in the uniforms. Tighter uniforms make it harder for opponents to grab hold of the jersey.

4 NFL uniforms are designed to be lightweight and breathable, so players can make great plays, and celebrate, with ease.

The Helmets

HORSESHOES ARE CONSIDERED A **GOOD LUCK** CHARM.

⌐ NFL helmets did not feature full facemasks until 1975.

Just like the uniforms, very little has changed about the Colts' helmet since 1957. The horseshoe **logo** is one of the most recognizable symbols in all of professional sports. From Unitas to Manning to Andrew Luck, it is almost impossible to picture the great Colts quarterbacks without thinking of the iconic blue horseshoe.

In the Colts' inaugural season of 1953, the helmets were blue with a white stripe. A new design to the Colts' helmet was introduced in 1954, but it only lasted a short time. For two seasons, the helmet was blue with a white stripe and a pair of white horseshoes appearing on the back. Then, in 1956, the colors were reversed. The helmets changed to white with a blue stripe and blue horseshoes. In 1957, the horseshoes moved to their current location on the helmet's sides. They have remained there ever since.

Shoulder pads were not commonly used in professional football until the 1950s.

The Coaches

CHUCKSTRONG

While Coach Chuck Pagano was undergoing leukemia treatment, two-dozen Colts players and two Colts cheerleaders shaved their heads in a show of support.

After 28 years of coaching, the Colts offered Chuck Pagano his first head-coaching job in the NFL.

Through the years, the Colts have followed many coaches to the height of professional football. Beginning with Weeb Ewbank, the coach who led the Colts to their first two NFL Championships, Colts coaches have been fair, good-tempered professionals who got the most out of their players.

DON SHULA

In 1963, the Colts hired 33-year-old Don Shula as head coach. In his second season in Baltimore, he led the Colts to a 12-2 record and was awarded Coach of the Year. He won this award a second time in 1968.

TONY DUNGY

In seven years as the head coach of the Indianapolis Colts, Tony Dungy won more games than any other Colts coach in team history. Each season he was there, the Colts made it to the playoffs. In February of 2006, Dungy became the first African American head coach to win a Super Bowl.

CHUCK PAGANO

In January of 2012, the Colts awarded Chuck Pagano his first NFL head-coaching job. The team was rebuilding, and Pagano knew that challenges lay ahead. In September of 2012, Pagano was diagnosed with leukemia and needed to take a break from his job. Pagano battled back from his illness, and in 2013, he led the Colts to an American Football Conference (AFC) South division title.

The Mascot

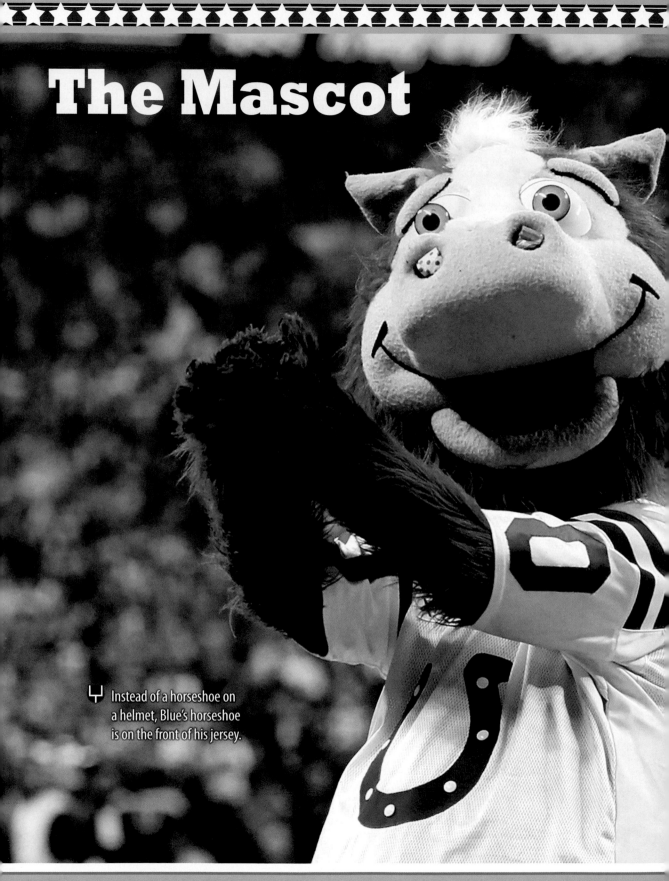

Instead of a horseshoe on a helmet, Blue's horseshoe is on the front of his jersey.

Blue the Mascot was a graduate of Jockey School in Stable, Indiana, where he excelled in football, track, wrestling, and dance. Blue then came to the Colts on September 17, 2006. Since his hiring, things have gone well for both the mascot and the team.

In Blue's first Colts game, they beat the Houston Texans 43-24, and it only got better from there. In Blue's first season as a member of the Colt family, the team won their first Super Bowl title in 36 years. In Blue's eight years of trotting up and down the sidelines, encouraging Colts fans to cheer their hearts out, the Colts have made the playoffs seven times.

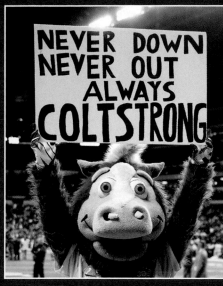

Blue is the Indianapolis Colts' biggest fan.

One of the highlights of Blue's career was opening for singer-songwriter Jimmy Buffett.

Legends of the Past

Many great players have suited up in the Colts' blue and white. A few of them have become icons of the team and the city it represents.

Johnny Unitas

Position Quarterback
Seasons 18 (1956–1973)
Born May 7, 1933, in Pittsburgh, Pennsylvania

Nicknamed "Johnny U" and "The Golden Arm," Johnny Unitas was the face of professional football for more than a decade. Despite his legendary status, Unitas never let fame get to his head. He famously said, "Conceit is bragging about yourself. Confidence means you believe you can get the job done." Unitas won four **most valuable player (MVP)** awards and leading the Colts to three NFL Championships in his hall of fame career. Unitas became the first NFL quarterback to pass for more than 3,000 yards in a season in 1960. He led the league in passing yards four times.

Edgerrin James

When Edgerrin James arrived in Indianapolis, he had some big shoes to fill. In his first season with the Colts, the University of Miami star was asked to replace future hall of fame running back Marshall Faulk. James exceeded all expectations. He led the NFL with 1,553 rushing yards, caught 62 passes for 586 yards, gained 2,139 **yards from scrimmage**, and was named Rookie of the Year. He followed that season up by setting a Colts record for yards from scrimmage (2,303) in 2000. In seven seasons with the Colts, James set the all-time franchise mark for rushing yards (9,226) and rushing touchdowns (64).

Position Running Back
Seasons 11 (1999–2009)
Born August 1, 1978, in Immokalee, Florida

Marvin Harrison

Peyton Manning and Marvin Harrison helped bring out the best in each other. They hold the record for most completions/receptions for a wide receiver/quarterback combination, with 953. Amongst numerous receiving records, Marvin Harrison holds the NFL record for most straight seasons with at least 10 touchdown receptions (8), and he is the only NFL receiver ever to top 1,400 yards in four straight seasons. Harrison retired an eight-time **Pro Bowler,** a member of the NFL 2000s All-Decade Team, and a Super Bowl champion.

Position Wide Receiver
Seasons 13 (1996–2008)
Born August 25, 1972, in Philadelphia, Pennsylvani

Peyton Manning

Peyton Manning was the face of the NFL in the 2000s. He appeared in football games and television commercials. Manning's ability to read defenses and give directions at the line of scrimmage made him one of the most feared quarterbacks in the league, and a near-impossible opponent to prepare for. In 13 seasons as the Colts' starting quarterback, Manning threw for a team-record 54,248 yards and 399 touchdowns. He registered a Colts-best 94.9 **passer rating**, made 11 Pro Bowls, led the team to an NFL-record nine straight playoff appearances, and won a Super Bowl.

Position Running Back
Seasons 15 (1998–2013)
Born March 24, 1976, in New Orleans, Louisiana

Stars of Today

Today's Colts team is made up of many young, talented players who have proven that they are among the best players in the league.

Andrew Luck

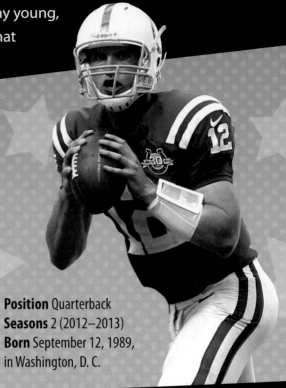

In recent memory, few athletes have started a professional career with higher expectations than Andrew Luck. As a two-time conference player of the year and an Academic All-American quarterback at Stanford University, Luck was viewed as a player with exceptional athletic skills and the intelligence to make the most of those gifts. As a member of the Colts, Andrew Luck has not disappointed. In two seasons, he tied the NFL record for most wins through 20 games (14), set the single-season record for rookie passing yards (4,374), set a rookie record for game-winning drives (7), and won an AFC South division title.

Position Quarterback
Seasons 2 (2012–2013)
Born September 12, 1989, in Washington, D. C.

Reggie Wayne

For many years now, Reggie Wayne quietly been establishing himself as one of the best wide receivers in NFL history. A favorite target of both Manning and Luck, Reggie Wayne broke into the starting line-up in 2003, teaming up with Marvin Harrison to become the most effective receiving duo in the league. Since Harrison's retirement in 2008, Wayne has not slowed down. In 2012, he had more than 1,000 receiving yards for the eighth time in his career. That same season, Wayne moved into second place on the all-time list for playoff receptions (92), trailing only hall of famer Jerry Rice.

Position Wide Receiver
Seasons 13 (2001–2013)
Born November 17, 1978, in New Orleans, Louisiana

Robert Mathis

During the 2013 season, Robert Mathis became the Colts' all-time **sacks** leader, passing former Colts linebacker Dwight Freeney. In the team's 14th game, he also broke Freeney's mark for most sacks in a single season with 16.5. No other Colt defender had more than five sacks through 14 games. Even though offenses never lost sight of him on the field, Mathis continued to dominate. With his record-breaking sack in Week 15, Mathis also stripped the ball from the opposing quarterback. The strip-sack was the 42nd of his career, an NFL record. Mathis finished the season with 19.5 sacks.

Position Defensive End/Linebacker
Seasons 11 (2003–2013)
Born February 26, 1981, in Atlanta, Georgia

T. Y. Hilton

After spending three seasons at Florida International University, T. Y. Hilton left the Sun Belt Conference to star on the largest stage in sports. In his rookie season with the Colts, Hilton caught 50 passes for 861 yards and seven touchdowns. He did this while averaging an impressive 17.2 yards per catch. At 5 feet, 9 inches and, 183 pounds, Hilton does not overwhelm opponents with his size. Instead, his abilities to stop quickly, change direction, and speed up allow him to extend each play, making him one of the most exciting players to wear a Colts' uniform.

Position Wide Receiver/Punt Returner
Seasons 2 (2012–2013)
Born November 14, 1989, in Miami, Florida

All-Time Records

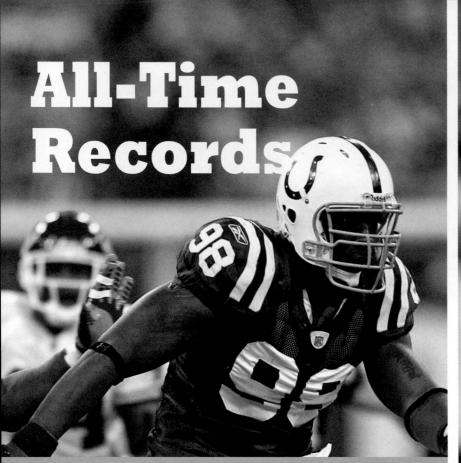

108
Career Sacks

Robert Mathis broke Dwight Freeney's Colts-record 107.5 career sacks in 2013.

54,828
All-time Passing Yards

Peyton Manning may one day break the NFL's all-time record for passing yards. In 13 seasons with the Indianapolis Colts, he passed for more than 4,000 yards in a season 11 times.

9,226 All-time Rushing Yards

Edgerrin James is the Colts' all-time rushing leader. In seven seasons with the Colts, he twice led the NFL in rushing.

85 **All-time Coaching Wins**

In just seven seasons as the Colts' head coach, Tony Dungy set the all-time mark for regular-season wins. His Colts averaged more than 12 wins per season.

14,580 **All-time Receiving Yards**

Marvin Harrison had more than 1,000 receiving yards each season for eight straight years between 1999 and 2006.

Timeline

Throughout the team's history, the Indianapolis Colts have had many memorable events that have become defining moments for the team and its fans.

1953
Owner Carroll Rosenbloom purchases the remains of the Dallas Texans franchise and founds a new team in Baltimore, Maryland. The team is named "Colts" after another professional football team that played in Baltimore from 1947 to 1951.

1970
The **American Football League (AFL)** and NFL **merge** and the Baltimore Colts join the American Football Conference (AFC). Johnny Unitas and Earl Morrall share the quarterback duties, but it is the Colts' outstanding defense that leads them to a win over the Dallas Cowboys in Super Bowl V.

The Colts win their third straight AFC East division title in 1977.

| 1955 | 1960 | 1965 | 1970 | 1975 | 1980 |

1958
Johnny Unitas, Lenny Moore, Alan Ameche, and Raymond Berry make up the league's best offense, and the Colts win the Western Division. Baltimore beats the New York Giants in the NFL Championship Game, 23-17, on a 1-yard run by Alan Ameche. The game is credited with creating nationwide interest in the NFL.

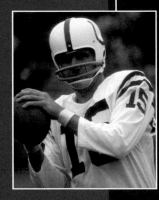

1968
Earl Morrall fills in for an injured Unitas and wins league MVP. The Colts NFL-best defense shuts down the Cleveland Browns in the NFL Championship Game, and the Colts win, 34-0.

1984
The Baltimore Colts move to Indianapolis, and in two weeks the team receives 143,000 requests for season tickets. In their first season in Indianapolis, the Colts go 4-12 and finish in fourth place in the AFC East.

The Future
Teams that win consistently in the NFL do it in many ways. They play tough on the road, win the turnover battle, and avoid penalties. They play smart, disciplined football and do not beat themselves. Above all, the key ingredient in every consistent winner is a great quarterback. With Andrew Luck, Colts fans can count on winning football for years to come.

1995
Nicknamed the "Cardiac Colts" because of all their close games, Colts quarterback Jim Harbaugh leads them to their first AFC Championship Game since 1971. In that game, the Colts come up just short, falling to Pittsburgh, 20-16.

In 2012, rookie quarterback Andrew Luck sets the NFL's rookie passing record.

| 1990 | 1995 | 2000 | 2005 | 2010 | 2015 |

In 1999, Manning leads the Colts to a 13-3 record and an AFC East division title.

February 4, 2007
In a battle against the Chicago Bears, Pro Bowl receivers Marvin Harrison and Reggie Wayne help Peyton Manning bring Indianapolis its first Super Bowl title. Tony Dungy becomes the first African American to coach an NFL team to a Super Bowl championship.

2013
In Chuck Pagano's first full year at the helm, he coaches the Colts to an AFC South division title. Despite a season-ending injury to Pro Bowler Reggie Wayne, Andrew Luck continues to shine. On the defensive side of the ball, Robert Mathis sets the Colts single-season sacks record.

Write a Biography

Life Story

A person's life story can be the subject of a book. This kind of book is called a biography. Biographies often describe the lives of people who have achieved great success. These people may be alive today, or they may have lived many years ago. Reading a biography can help you learn more about a great person.

Get the Facts

Use this book, and research in the library and on the Internet, to find out more about your favorite Colt. Learn as much about this player as you can. What position does he play? What are his statistics in important categories? Has he set any records? Also, be sure to write down key events in the person's life. What was his childhood like? What has he accomplished off the field? Is there anything else that makes this person special or unusual?

Use the Concept Web

A concept web is a useful research tool. Read the questions in the concept web on the following page. Answer the questions in your notebook. Your answers will help you write a biography.

Concept Web

Adulthood
- Where does this individual currently reside?
- Does he or she have a family?

Your Opinion
- What did you learn from the books you read in your research?
- Would you suggest these books to others?
- Was anything missing from these books?

Childhood
- Where and when was this person born?
- Describe his or her parents, siblings, and friends.
- Did this person grow up in unusual circumstances?

Accomplishments off the Field
- What is this person's life's work?
- Has he or she received awards or recognition for accomplishments?
- How have this person's accomplishments served others?

Write a Biography

Help and Obstacles
- Did this individual have a positive attitude?
- Did he or she receive help from others?
- Did this person have a mentor?
- Did this person face any hardships?
- If so, how were the hardships overcome?

Accomplishments on the Field
- What records does this person hold?
- What key games and plays have defined his or her career?
- What are his or her stats in categories important to his or her position?

Work and Preparation
- What was this person's education?
- What was his or her work experience?
- How does this person work; what is the process he or she uses?

Trivia Time

Take this quiz to test your knowledge of the Indianapolis Colts. The answers are printed upside-down under each question.

1 Who is the Colts' all-time sacks leader?

A. Robert Mathis

2 Which Colts coach led the team to a win in a Super Bowl?

A. Tony Dungy

3 Who holds the Colts' record for all-time passing yards?

A. Peyton Manning

4

A. 1984

5 What were the nicknames given to Colts hall of famer Johnny Unitas?

A. "Johnny U" and "The Golden Arm"

6 Which Colts quarterback holds the NFL's rookie passing record with 4,374 yards?

A. Andrew Luck

7 Which Colts receiver set an NFL record with four straight seasons of more than 1,400 receiving yards?

A. Marvin Harrison

8 Which Colts coach led the team to back-to-back NFL Championships?

A. Weeb Ewbank

9 The Colts tied an NFL record in the 2000s by making the playoffs in how many straight seasons?

A. Nine

10 What year did the Colts' horseshoe helmets make their first appearance?

A. 1957

Key Words

.500: when a team wins and loses an equal number of games. In the NFL, an 8-8 win-loss record is a .500 season

American Football League (AFL): major American Professional Football league that operated from 1960 until 1969, when it merged with the National Football League (NFL)

hall of fame: a group of persons judged to be outstanding, as in a sport or profession

inaugural: marking the beginning of an institution, activity, or period of office

logo: a symbol that stands for a team or organization

merge: a combination of two leagues or teams into one

Most Valuable Player (MVP): the player judged to be most valuable to his team's success

NFL Draft: an annual event where the NFL chooses college football players to be new team members

passer rating: a rating given to quarterbacks that tries to measure how well they perform on the field

playoffs: the games played following the end of the regular season. Six teams are qualified: the four winners of the different conferences, and the two best teams that did not finish first in their respective conference (the wild cards)

Pro Bowler: NFL players who take part in the annual all-star game that pits the best players in the National Football Conference against the best players in the American Football Conference

retractable: a retractable roof can move from an open position into a closed or extended position that completely covers the field of play and spectator areas

sacks: a sack occurs when the quarterback is tackled behind the line of scrimmage before he can throw a forward pass

Super Bowl: the NFL's annual championship game between the winning team from the NFC and the winning team from the AFC

yards from scrimmage: the total of rushing yards and receiving yards from the yard-line on the field from which the play starts

Index

Log on to www.av2books.com

AV² by Weigl brings you media enhanced books that support active learning. Go to www.av2books.com, and enter the special code found on page 2 of this book. You will gain access to enriched and enhanced content that supplements and complements this book. Content includes video, audio, weblinks, quizzes, a slide show, and activities.

AV² Online Navigation

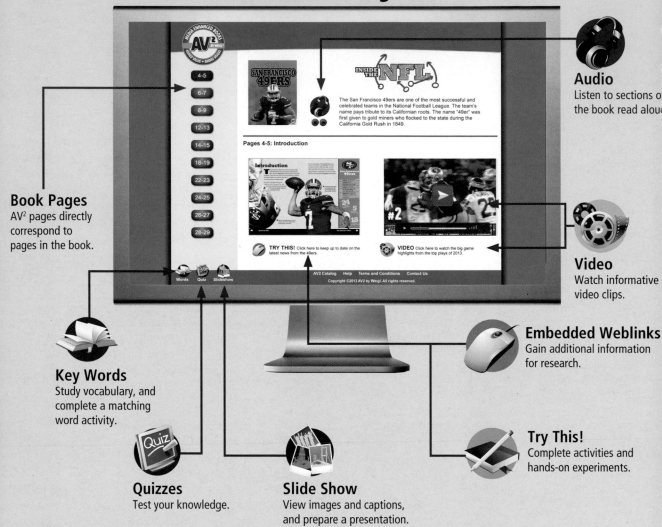

Audio
Listen to sections of the book read aloud

Book Pages
AV² pages directly correspond to pages in the book.

Video
Watch informative video clips.

Key Words
Study vocabulary, and complete a matching word activity.

Embedded Weblinks
Gain additional information for research.

Try This!
Complete activities and hands-on experiments.

Quizzes
Test your knowledge.

Slide Show
View images and captions, and prepare a presentation.

AV² was built to bridge the gap between print and digital. We encourage you to tell us what you like and what you want to see in the future.

Sign up to be an AV² Ambassador at www.av2books.com/ambassador.